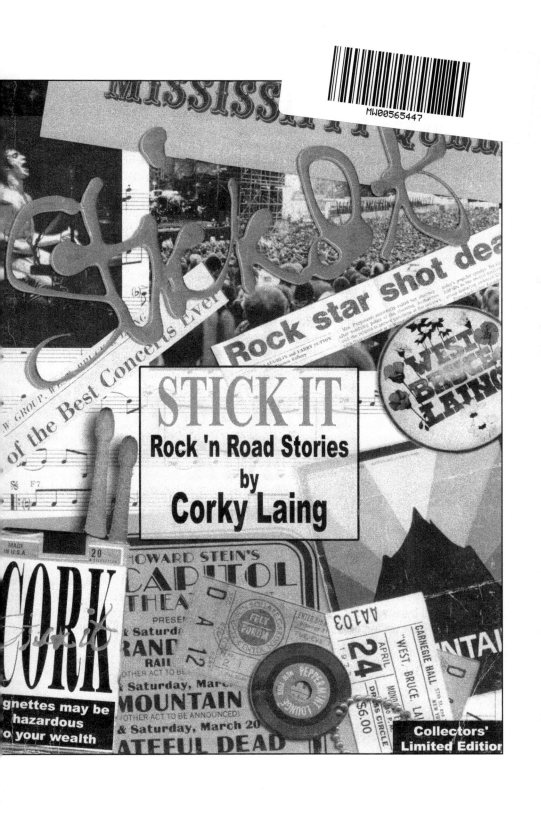

Edited and scanned by Andrea Rider, Corinna Downes
Typeset by Jonathan Downes
Cover and original layout by Stephen Ibbott
This edition - layout by SPiderKaT for CFZ Communications
Using Microsoft Word 2000, Microsoft Publisher 2000, Adobe Photoshop CS.

First self published in Canada
Second edition by Gonzo Multimedia 2014

c/o Brooks City,
6th Floor New Baltic House,
65 Fenchurch Street,
London EC3M 4BE
**Fax:** +44 (0)191 5121104
**Tel:** +44 (0) 191 5849144
**International Numbers:**
**Germany:** Freephone 08000 825 699
**USA:** Freephone 18666 747 289

© Gonzo Multimedia MMXIV

## ISBN: 978-1-908728-41-8

# FORELWORD
# by Levon Helm

Of all the lead guitar trios of the 1970's, Jimi Hendrix Experience, Cream, and Mountain come to mind first. As the drummer for Mountain, Corky Laing shares the title as one of the best players of that genre.

He's also the same good guy he used to be. Tell the truth and stay strong my brother.

**L.H.**
**Woodstock, N.Y. 2001**

"As the drummer for Mountain, Corky Laing shares the title as one of the best players of that genre."

# Acknowledgements

The Author would like to thank the following people for their generous support and participation

Carol, Leslie, Jeffrey, & Stephen Laing, Earl and Alden Shuman, Gail & Terry Coen, Mr. & Mrs. Leslie West, Midnight Ramble Crew, Barbara O'Brian, Marty Schwartz & Gail, Bill Brownstein, Kinky Friedman, Don Imus, Leni Laing, Ratso, Bob Brennan, Mick Brigden, David Grahame, Len Blum, George Risanyl, Eric Schenkman, Tito, Charlie Karp, Noel Redding, Richard Bennett, Bob Kirsch, Tutti, Mr. & Mrs. David Hostetler, Jerry Mall, Kostas, Gary Lyons, Roy Pike, Taffi Rosen, Howie Altholtz, Paul Barkley, Mr. & Mrs. Peter Demilio, Tutt, Jay & Jerry Tormey, Larry Pelligrini, Sylvain (At Maestro), Jack Tepperman, David Steinberg, Steve Ship, Dr. Satok, also Josh & Yvonne Horton, Aldo and Mellenie, Keith & Anastasia, Dale Suter and Heather, Gary Hygrin, Denny Colt, Bonnie Parker, Tuija Takala, Matti Hayrey, Mirris and Risto Takala (and all the Finnish Gang who are "Playing God"), Melissa and John Shea, Kate Mueth and Josh Gladston @ Guild Hall, Rob Ayling, Andrea Rider, Corinna Downes, Jonathan Downes, Dave Barker, Chris Barrie, David Balcon, Jack & Malcolm Bruce, Larry & Teressa Campbell, Elliott Rubinson, Steve @ Evans Drumheads, Peter Spamanato, Laila, Mikel, & Val, Mell & Clive, The Rosen Family, Tom & Dr. Jacqueline Greenwood.

It's not how big the stick is, it's how it is handled

# Introduction

**Y**ou know the joke: The drummer is a guy who hangs out with musicians. Well, it's not too far from the truth. Usually the better the musicians a drummer is hanging with, the better drummer he will become. I owe whatever kind of drummer I am to the people in these stories. Please forgive the name-dropping aspect of this book; this mandate was set when I first sat down on the drum throne.

I've always considered the University of Rock a spiritual institution; in the Temple of Groove and Feel with the Muse as the Master.

When graduating from this institute, one is thrown into the jungle of Ego, Greed and Deception. Despite these experiences, one may not, cannot and will not count on money as compensation. You're considered a success if you can live an honest day by playing music.

However, the perks are sometimes special. Not only do you get your T-shirts and posters, you also get to meet some of the most amazing people. And there are also those great 'road stories'…

**My First Kit**

The Rolling Stones' first tour of North America; photographed here with *Bartholomew Plus 3*.

# In the Beginning:
# Bartholemew Plus 3 = Energy

## Growing up in a group

I was born into a group and have continued to live my life in a group. My older triplet brothers Leslie, Jeffrey, Steve and I slept in a small room in two double bunk beds. The four of us spent the better part of fifteen years playing hockey, basketball and sleeping as a group. I believe this is where I learned how to survive in a group - with many different attitudes, preferences and basic instincts. I enjoyed these early times. I was one of a gang and I had to be as good or better than the others in order to stay in the fold.

My sister, who was five years older, was the artist, musician and scholar in the family. She kept to herself and taught me basically to mind my own business - a good lesson indeed.

And since my Mom and Dad loved to dance and hang out till the late hours in the kitchen beside our bedroom, it all added up to a pretty good environment for me. Together, it made for a natural development: to learn to play drums, to keep up musically with better musicians, while minding my own business, and hanging out till the wee hours dancing and jiving. I always feel deeply indebted to my family; my brothers and sister are great friends and wonderful people.

Although I still think they have no idea what their little brother does for a living.

**Bartholemew Plus 3**

**THIRTY YEARS LATER AT NUREMBERG:**
**Having a few people over for a jam. What a job!**
**(Photo from the 'best seat in the house')**

As I said to Leslie, this was "Two Jews and a German (Rudolph Schenker) on stage at the site of the Nuremberg Rally, in front of a million youths. I don't think Hitler would have approved!"

"If you're gonna start something, the beginning is a hell of a good idea."

Sid Vicious,
USA Tour 1978

"Summer of '61 is when it all begun".

Corky Laing
2001

> **The Ink Spots** were an American vocal group popular in the 1930s and 1940s. Their music led to the rhythm and blues and rock and roll musical genres, and the subgenre doo-wop. The group was widely accepted in both the white and black communities, largely due to the ballad style introduced to the group by lead singer Bill Kenny. The group was inducted into the Rock & Roll Hall of Fame in 1999.

Any job was a good job when you were working at a Summer Cabana Club: out in the countryside, beautiful weather, beautiful view, beautiful women and a large stage with a beautiful white drum set.

My job was to keep them both clean and ready for the performers every night. They called me "Stage Manager". A musician's union strike had begun earlier that summer season. One evening, when the *Ink Spots* were the special guests, there was no back-up band for them.

At the last minute, the *Ink Spots* spotted me on the drums tightening, tuning 'em. They asked me if I could just give them a little cool time on the kit when they were performing.

I was too scared to say no and too stupid to say yes. There I was, 13 years old, performing with the legendary *Ink Spots* - my very first gig. Four beautiful black men with the smoothest harmonies and velvet voices, backed up by a little white kid on drums who, in fact, had just finished sweeping the stage.

What a beautiful moment to jump start a career.

"What a beautiful moment to jump start a career".

"STANDELLS"

The Standells are a garage rock band from Los Angeles, California, US, formed in the 1960s, who have been referred to as the "punk band of the 1960's", and said to have inspired such groups as the Sex Pistols and Ramones. They are best known for their 1966 hit "Dirty Water", now the anthem of several Boston

When John Lennon and Yoko Ono stopped in Montreal during their Bed-In for Peace tour, I just had to meet them. Along with fake newspaper reporter ID, my bass player buddy George, and a great deal of chutzpah, I stood in line at the Queen Elizabeth Hotel wondering if I could actually pull this off.

George, as it turned out, hadn't brought ID and got left behind. But there I was, second in line, about to meet the famous couple. However, things started going downhill when the fellow in front of me managed to really piss John off. He had tried to sell the former Beatle a poster, made from a photograph he had taken the day before, of John and Yoko in bed. And he was asking $15,000 for it! John just blew up and screamed, "Throw the SOB of a French Pepsi out!

What a fuckin' nerve - trying to sell me, me and Yoko."

I was next in line and boy was I fudging my silks. What the fuck do I say? John was pissed!  As their manager directed me into their room, to the seat beside John and Yoko's bed, I was doing everything I could to collect myself.  I couldn't believe I had made it this far in the first place. "John", I said (in a very full-of-shit voice), "I'm really sorry, but I'm not a newspaper writer, I'm just a musician in a local band who would do anything to meet you. I'll just leave. . ." and started to get up.

"Whoa," John shot right back.

Sit down a minute. I've got to cool down anyway. Maybe talking to a musician is a good idea. So, what's the story?"

Well", I replied, "I'm a drummer in a band called *Energy*".

e nudged Yoko, "Eh Yoko, what a great name for a band. *Energy*, yeah, very cool."

s we talked about songs and writing, I noticed the poster the Frenchman had left behind. It ad: 'Hair Peace.' I said, "You know, it's really not that bad of an idea. Would you mind if I ept it?"

You do have a set of balls Mr. Energy," John said. "Yeah take it, but not until we sign it to nergy". So they did.

ears later, when John and I crossed paths in the Record Plant Studios, (I sang background on s "Rock and Roll" album) we had a good laugh about this day. Too bad the band *Energy* asn't as memorable as the name.

**Gary Ship, me and George Gardos (formerly B+3) = *Energy***

BILL GRAHAM PRESENTS IN NEW YORK

## Tuesday Night New Groups

EVERY WEEK AT 8.00 P.M.
3 NEW GROUPS
3 NEW LIGHT SHOWS
– $1.50 at the Door

FRIDAY & SATURDAY, MARCH 27 & 28

### JOE COCKER
#### The GREASE BAND
BRIAN AUGER & THE TRINITY
STONE THE CROWS

FRIDAY & SATURDAY, APRIL 3 & 4

### QUICKSILVER
MESSENGER SERVICE

### VAN MORRISON

SUNDAY, APRIL 5 – 8.00 PM

### TOM PAXTON
ONLY NEW YORK APPEARANCE

FRI., SAT. & SUN., APRIL 10, 11 & 12

### SANTANA
IT'S A BEAUTIFUL DAY
FREE

FRIDAY & SATURDAY, APRIL 17 & 18

### RAY CHARLES
& HIS ORCHESTRA
with
THE RAELETTES

### DIZZY GILLESPIE
QUINTET

### MONGO SANTAMARIA

THURSDAY, APRIL 23 AT 8.00 PM
FRIDAY & SATURDAY, APRIL 24 & 25
SUNDAY, APRIL 26 AT 7.00 PM

### "U"
– a Pop Pantomime
presented by
### The INCREDIBLE STRING BAND
THE STONE MONKEY MIME TROUPE

TUESDAY & WEDNESDAY, APRIL 28 & 29

### JEFFERSON AIRPLANE
#### MANFRED MANN
CHAPTER THREE

FRIDAY & SATURDAY, MAY 1 & 2

### MOUNTAIN

FRIDAY & SATURDAY, MAY 8 & 9

### MOTHERS OF INVENTION
with
### FRANK ZAPPA
The NICE

FRIDAY & SATURDAY, MAY 29 & 30

### NINA SIMONE

FRIDAY thru SUNDAY, JUNE 2 thru 3

### CROSBY–STILLS –NASH & YOUNG

JOSHUA LIGHT SHOW

## FILLMORE EAST
SECOND AVENUE AT SIXTH STREET

# My son the drummer

My mother, Sarah, God bless her, was very proud when I began playing the big New York City gigs, like the Fillmore East and Carnegie Hall. One night, I got her the best seats in the house: the balcony overlooking the stage. What I didn't know was Mom was sitting beside Jimi Hendrix and his girlfriend, with Bob Dylan on her other side. Jimi later told me that Sarah was "very polite."

At one point, Jimi's girlfriend began dancing right in front of her. Sarah turned to Jimi and said: "Would you please ask your girlfriend to dance aside so I can see my son?"

For some reason they just 'clicked'. Jimi thought she was cute. She thought Jimi was cute and they both had a laugh when some kid from Montreal screamed out, "Hey Laing, two minutes for tripping." I thought the hockey reference was about the Montreal Canadians jersey that I was wearing that night on stage. However, I was soon to find out the 'other' meaning to the joke...

"The trouble with this Rock & Roll music biz is, when you finally do something (get a hit, etc), and finally get some money, it is seven minutes too late to really mean anything".

Lowell George

## Two gold records
Were you at Woodstock or were you too straight to remember?

Here's a real pisser. I'm sitting on the beach in Nantucket with my good buddy Nick Ferrantella, the very first day of Woodstock weekend. I had just come back from New York where Felix Pappalardi and Leslie West were rehearsing a song for *Mountain's* Woodstock performance (they were known then as *Leslie West's Mountain*). They were going to play

**By the time they got to Woodstock they were half a million strong**

Who Am I but You and the Sun," which had been written originally by my band *Energy* (with Gary Ship and George Gardos).

Felix, who had been producing *Energy*, loved the song. I was thrilled that they had chosen one of our tunes and felt I was at least going to be at Woodstock 'spiritually'. While in New York, the week before, Felix asked me if I'd like to do him a favour: check on some new drum kits at Manny's place and get him the info.

Fast forward to December 1969; enter naive Corky (Canadian-born-totally-impressed-with-everything) Laing! There I was at the Record Plant still hoping to be at Woodstock - even though Woodstock had been in August earlier that year. I was commissioned by the band *Ten Years After* to put drums on their live, Woodstock version of "Goin' Home" (all twenty-two minutes of it). The drum microphones for Rick Lee (the original drummer) had broken down during that performance and the drums were missing on the live track. As history will note,

"Anything that can be played soft, can be played loud." Felix

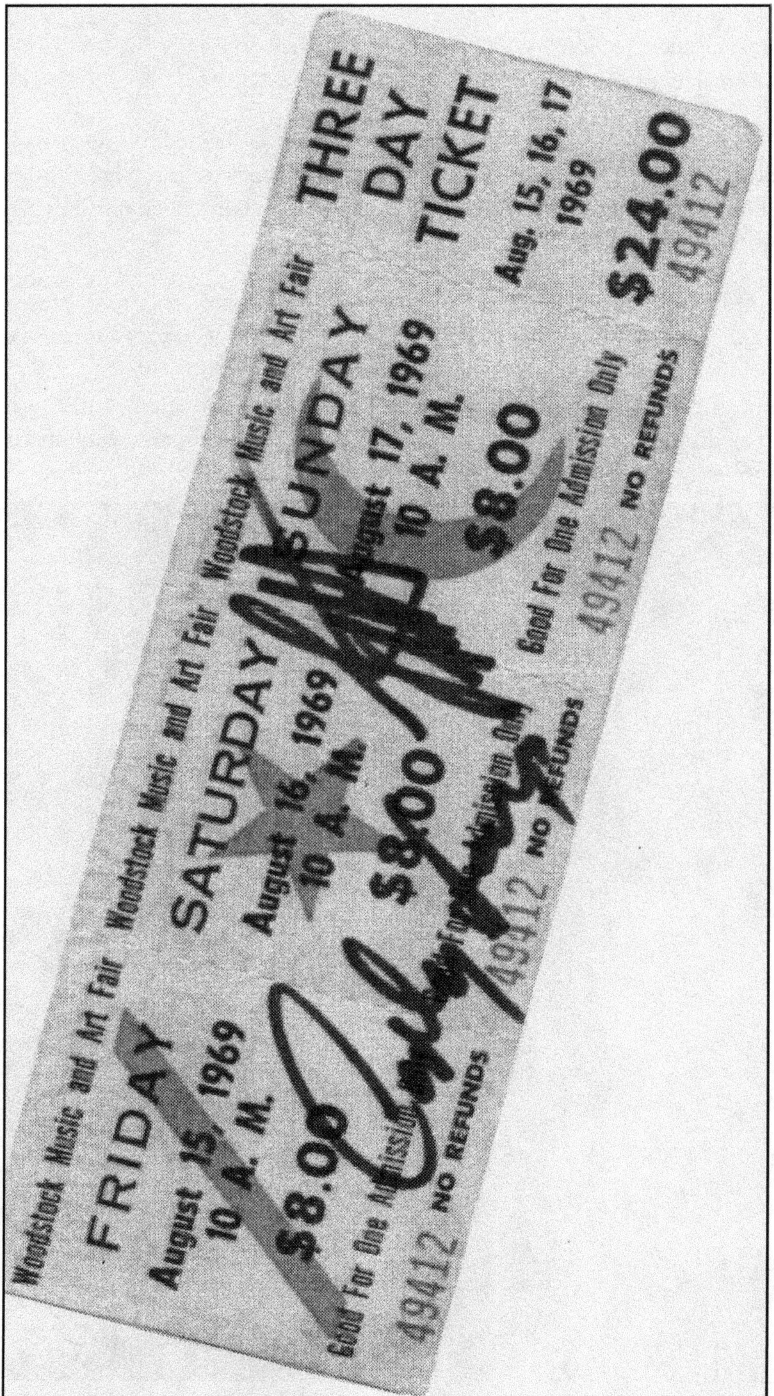
Woodstock Music and Art Fair
FRIDAY
August 15, 1969
10 A. M.
$8.00
Good For One Admission Only
NO REFUNDS
49412
SATURDAY
August 16, 1969
10 A. M.
$8.00
Good For One Admission Only
NO REFUNDS
49412
SUNDAY
August 17, 1969
10 A. M.
$8.00
Good For One Admission Only
NO REFUNDS
49412
THREE DAY TICKET
Aug. 15, 16, 17
1969
$24.00
49412

this song became the *HIT* on the Woodstock Album. It immediately went Gold in the summer of 1970.

Let me tell you, it was hard to keep time with Alvin Lee on "Goin' Home". Probably some of my most ambitious drumming I ever did, except for the months I played with *Meatloaf*. The song was over twenty minutes long and was like following a runaway train that had PMS.

In the end though, I received a gold record for playing with *Ten Years After*, and another gold record for *Mountain's* version of "Yasgur's Farm", the title of which had been changed from "Who Am I but You and the Sun."

I got two gold records from Woodstock and I wasn't even there!

# for yasgur's farm

words and music by george gardos, corky laing,
felix pappalardi-gail collins,
gary ship, david rea

recorded by
mountain
on windfall records

# for yasgur's farm

Words and Music by
GEORGE GARDOS, CORKY LAING,
FELIX PAPPALARDI, GAIL COLLINS
GARY SHIP and DAVID REA

      G     /    D   /    Em /// C   /    D    /    Em  ///
Who am         ou and the sun,    a slight reflection of ev'ryone.

C /              /      Bm /
Was it            away?

                        B ///
Were               me?

    G
Wha

C

    T

C

Chorus:                                                 /
                                                ou.

                                                 B ///
    Em                                              y and lies.
Chorus: Look at me,                                 /     D /
                                          a part of you.

    G    /    D
Quiet as the voices in a d

C    /        D     /
Without you, shadowed, the things I'v

C    /         D   /   Em    /    Bm
Remember the evening I let you walk away?

       C    /     B♭°  /       B ///
Were you the one, or is it we're the same?

       Em  ///    G     ///           A7   /// C   /     D / G(hold
Chorus: Look at me, I believe the truth. You're a part of me, I'm a part of you.

Note: In order to play along with the record, capo up 2 frets.

## Marilyn in my Chambers

When I first joined up with Mountain, I took over Felix and Gail's old apartment in Greenwich Village. Since it was my first very own "Love Nest", I had some erotic design ideas. The back bedroom would be all bed. Wall-to-wall bed.

To give it a Mediterranean look, I stuccoed the walls. I had a hard time with the plaster though and instead of a rustic smooth surface I ended up with very jagged edges sticking out like horizontal stalagmites. They were very sharp-edged walls. And because we were in-and-out of town on tour so much, I had to leave smoothing them down until time allowed.

Returning from some California gig, I was introduced to a very young and innocent-looking actress named Marilyn Chambers. She had just finished a small part in the Barbara Streisand movie, *Owl and the Pussycat*. Rich Totoyion, our promo man, told me that he had met her on the train from Westport and that she was dying to meet a Rock & Roll drummer. Here I was, ready, willing and able.

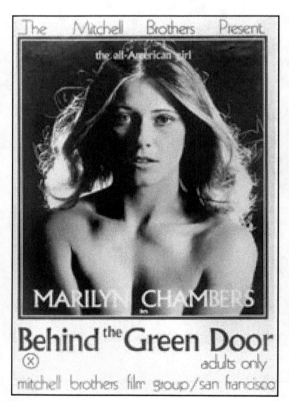

The Mitchell Brothers Present
the all-American girl
MARILYN CHAMBERS
Behind the Green Door
ⓧ adults only
mitchell brothers film group / san francisco

Finally, when push came to shove, she shoved her love into my dark bedroom and we went at it. Or should I say she went at it.

I just tried to hold on to it.

After what seemed to be hours (yeah, sure) I looked up at her, since she was on top, and saw that she was covered in blood! She must have been scratching her arms and back against my cutting-edge stucco walls. And I don't think she had even noticed, let alone cared.

Her eyes were closed and she just kept on wiping the blood all over her as she rode me until the weekend was over (or was it the week). Afterward, she just threw her bloodied shirt over her blood-smeared body and jumped out of the bloody bed, never to be seen again by me - till the release of her movie: *Behind the (*Bloody*) Green Door*.

## Ridin' naked

During those days of love and drug experiments, one didn't know if it was charm, money, or good looks that made a woman do the things she would do. For instance, I was once out in the Vermont countryside visiting my artist buddy, Roy Bailey, when from out of nowhere a beautiful blonde rode up on a horse, looking, perhaps, a little dazed. It was cocktail hour and being in the spirit of things, Roy and I naturally started to goof on her a little.

In an effort to convince Roy that she should pose for him and would make a wonderful Lady

Godiva, she said she wanted to audition by taking off all her clothes and ride around nude. Since it was a freezing cold winter afternoon, Roy politely invited her inside where there was a welcoming warm fireplace aglow. But she declined and insisted she audition outdoors in the bright daylight, on the snowy roadway, in the thirty degrees below zero weather. And she asked me to accompany her since her horse was 'skid-ish' on the icy roads. We tried to convince her not to do it (for at least two seconds) - it was too cold to ride naked through the woods - but she insisted.

Only then, did we realize it was not our charm (or whatever good looks we had) that prompted this 'you had to be there' moment. She was totally stoned on LSD. Covered in a Buffalo coat, I accompanied the beautiful naked woman as she rode through the forest up to Roy's cottage. When we arrived, I dismounted, hoping she might too. But no, she just kept on going eventually disappearing into the sunset.

Lady Godiva, what a beautiful sight, and never to be seen by either of us again.

# MISSISSIPPI QUEEN

Words and Music by
LESLIE WEST, CORKY LAING, FELIX PAPPALARDI, DAVID REA

# The truth about the Queen

It was the summer of '69, it was hot, it was sweaty, it was at a beach club in Nantucket called 30 Acres. Everyone who owned an air conditioner in Nantucket must have switched them on because at 12:30 am that Saturday night the master fuse blew the juice.

Energy, my band, was a self-contained trio (bass, keyboards, and drums) and we took great pride on writing our own songs. We also took a lot of soul pills to keep the casual glow over our six 40-minute sets. Anyway on this night, we were jamming, they were dancin', and it was hot, sorta soft porn hot. My artist-buddy Roy Bailey was dancin' with a gorgeous southern babe, Molly, and I couldn't take my eyes off her and her see-through, flower-print, skin-tight dress. She was grindin' and humpin', and I was thumpin' and starin'. Bingo 12:30 - the juice goes out, there was a power outage on the entire island, and the band except for Corky are suddenly unplugged. But no way was I stoppin' and losin' Molly on the dance floor.

I started smashing the cowbell a la cha-cha-cha and with the help of the soul pills I started streamin' Mississippi Queen in honour of Molly - from the south. "Mississippi Queen do you know what I mean? Do you know what I mean, Molly?" She looked at me with this beautiful southern smile and she knew exactly what I meant. That night the song continued conservatively for over an hour; until the electricity came back on. So by the end of the night, Roy got laid, and I had a tune, (recorded on a friend's tape machine). We made a record, had a hit, and then I got laid.

P.S. I made the record with the help of Leslie West's unbelievable lick. I know he started getting laid too.

P.S.S. Jimi Hendrix was the first person to hear the final mix of the Queen and it turned him on to Mountain immediately.

# Busted in the Rockies

Mountain loved Denver and the Rockies and vice versa. I guess you could say it was a fit. The day after we had performed an outstanding gig with the Blues image, we all took 'time off' and we really meant 'off'. We usually got off any way we could.

In my case, I hooked up with a quintessential Hippie chick: real cute, great body, didn't shave, didn't bathe etc. She invited me to Boulder to go horseback riding. On my arrival at the foothills, I found myself in a cult commune, you know, holding hands - um, um, um  veggies - um, um, um - holding hands - um, um, um.

I can't wait to get out of here - um, um, um. What did I get myself into - um, um, um.  I finally turned to her and said "Rosie, let's get the fuck out of here and ride."

So Rosie and I are getting high riding in the Rockies. I think I ate my first 'shroom 'because I began to get a bit paranoid. You know, out in the middle of the Rockies, riding a strange horse, along with a strange hippie chick, who made love in very strange positions.

At one point on the ride, during a "love rest", I started imagining she was looking at the horse in a very 'strange' way. "Noooo way," I said. "No sloppy-seconds after a horse. Let's start back."

*Mountain* in the Rocky Mountains with a mountain of Sun amps behind us (a monumental performance)

The paranoia got worse and just as I began talking myself down from this feeling I hear a helicopter overhead. It is a Police helicopter, in the middle of the Rocky Mountains, and I have no doubt he's coming after me. I start to piss myself, 'What the Hell?'

Then the electric megaphone: "Are you Corky Laing? Signal if you are Corky Laing!"

I'm busted! I can't believe this! They are busting me in the middle of a horseback ride! Shaking, I try to discretely check my pockets for anything illegal. "If you are Corky Laing, proceed down to the trail to the access road. A patrol car will meet you," blares the megaphone.

I'm screwed, it's all over, Rosie's an informant... all this is going through my blood-pulsing brain. What else could I do, I was busted.

Then it occurred to me - for what?

When I approached the patrol car, the Colorado State Trooper informed me they were looking all over for me because *Mountain* (the band) had agreed to do an open-air charity concert at Boulder University that afternoon. I was free (and so was the concert). I bid farewell to my hippie-lover, leaving her to take care of the two horses (hmmm...) - and tore off to Boulder University for the show.

# Plane crash

Since Felix despised the introduction of electronic frisking at the airports, he began to consider private jets for touring. All we needed were multiple gigs per day and he would secure for us a Learjet. But in truth, our tour schedule had become so gruelling by that point we really did have to travel by private Jet.

On the occasion of our first headline arena date in Cleveland, we were joined on the trip by the elite core of *Mountain's* agents and managers. I believe we even moved up to a Gulfstream jet to take on the heavies like Leslie West and agent Frank Barsalona. Bud Prager (manager), Mary Beth (road manager), Felix, Gail and myself were also on board.

We had just taken off from Tetaboro Airport in New Jersey when the pilot informed us there could be trouble. The landing gear was not operating properly. It was impossible to fly all the way to Cleveland with the landing gear exposed, so we headed to Philly instead. We were going to 'buzz' the airport tower there in the hopes that the air-traffic controllers could spot and solve the problem. Needless to say, all of the passengers, including myself were getting pretty edgy.

There was nothing the controllers could do so the resolve was to execute an emergency landing, meaning: line up the fire trucks, foam the runway. We gonna crash land!

During the runway preparation, we had to jettison the fuel. There was no turning back now. Without going into detail, all grown men were crying, Gail and Mary Beth were whining, and I just couldn't believe I was going to die in a plane crash.

However, great moments were flashing before my eyes: Marilyn Chambers, Marilyn Chambers and Marilyn Chambers.

Although there were no embarrassing confessions (as in the movie, "'Almost Famous" ) when our final descent was imminent, there were a lot of "I really love you guys" between the tears. We crashed down on the faulty landing gear and the plane shimmied all over the place till it came to a standstill. Then the tears really started to be shed - tears of joy.

There is a humorous side to this story, sort of.

The news of our crash (before it happened) was all over Cleveland and there were hours of delay before the music industry found out that *Mountain* had survived. We were presumed dead to certain insiders in the biz. To this day, I'm still not sure if we were missed. And we never did reschedule that show in Cleveland.

Mountain and crew touring in a city bus during the airline strike.

# The Festival Express

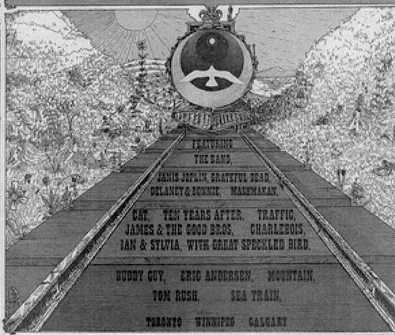

1970 1970

EATON-WALKER ASSOCIATES LIMITED

presents

# TRANS CONTINENTAL POP FESTIVAL

FEATURING

THE BAND,

JANIS JOPLIN, GRATEFUL DEAD,

DELANEY & BONNIE, MASHMAKAN,

CAT, TEN YEARS AFTER, TRAFFIC,
JAMES & THE GOOD BROS., CHARLEBOIS,
IAN & SYLVIA, WITH GREAT SPECKLED BIRD,

BUDDY GUY, ERIC ANDERSEN, MOUNTAIN,

TOM RUSH, SEA TRAIN,

TORONTO WINNIPEG CALGARY

Cut along dotted line and mail

With Money Order or Certified Cheque
**FESTIVAL EXPRESS 1970**

(NAME) ............................................

(ADDRESS) ........................................

(NUMBER OF TICKETS)

1 DAY ☐
SAT. ☐   SUN. ☐
$8 EACH DAY

2 DAYS ☐
$14

Mail this coupon to any of the ticket outlets listed.

**TORONTO**
JUNE 27 & 28 — CNE GRANDSTAND
(NOON TO MIDNIGHT EACH DAY)

MAIL ORDER — CNE BOX OFFICE

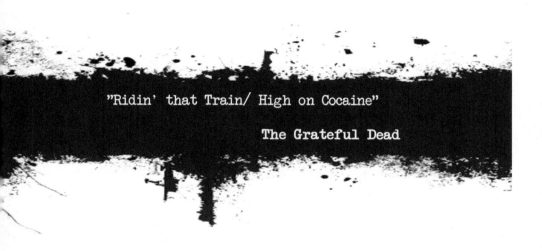

"Ridin' that Train/ High on Cocaine"

The Grateful Dead

The great Festival Express Train included every major music artist of the 1970's. The only problem was every act had to stay on board the train while it made its way across Canada. It took ten days! Except for the dining car and the bar car, all the musicians were pretty much confined to their own quarters.

I think the Toronto show was enhanced when Janis Joplin's birthday cake was spiced with LSD. Backstage was a show in itself. I remember Van Morrison freaking out because no one told him about the LSD. In those days you could count on every kind of drug being used in drinks and brownies.

You had to watch what you ate in order not to miss the trip. Seriously, the problem with the Festival Express Train was that musicians aren't a lot of fun when they are trapped - and that's how we all started feeling after the first night. As a matter of fact, I don't think any of the Mountain Peaking groups lasted aboard the train more than a couple nights.

The very first night in Montreal, Leslie and I set up our mini-equipment to do a little practice. Before we knew it, in came The Dead, *The Band*, Bonnie and Delaney. Within minutes it felt that every guitar in Canada was blaring out of the bar car. The fact that we all complained about the lack of medicinal inspiration did not affect the music.

In truth, we were all lying - we were hiding it, not dividing it.

When we pulled through small towns in beautiful rural areas, townspeople would gather and greet the Festival Express with welcome signs, etc. At one such stop in Ontario, I was joined by a beautiful lady, a PR agent, who I had met earlier that month during a brief promotional stint.

We spent that evening on board in my private roomette and were totally oblivious to the sun beginning to rise as we pulled into Sarnia. And we were also oblivious to the fact that the roomette, when open, was at the same level as the train's window. My ass (and my beautiful partner) were totally exposed and in perfect view of the 100 or so townspeople of Sarnia.

The people were hysterical, giving me a rousing, or should I say a rousing round of applause. My PR woman refused to surface for a curtain call. Her face was as red as the sunrise.

This inspired me to write a clever (though unreleased) little tune called "Moon over Sarnia".

ABOVE: (Left) Jerry Garcia  (Right)  Quebec's Bob Dylan Robert Charlebois

OPPOSITE: (Above) Festival Express party (Below) Keeping an eye on Janis from under my 10-gallon cowboy hat.

**Janis Joplin and friends**

# Celeb surprise party

When Leslie and I were in between millions, management decided it was time for a Leslie West solo album. During the recording sessions, various musicians would drop by and lend a hand writing and playing. Mick Jagger, for instance, contributed to a tune or two for what would become the Great Fatsby album.

Meanwhile, Leslie's thirtieth birthday had arrived and I decided to throw a surprise party for him at our Manager's Central Park penthouse suite.

Trying not to seem too presumptuous, I invited Mick and asked if he knew of any other music celebs (so to speak) who could join up.

"What? He sneered back, "I'm not good enough?"

After a bit of a giggle over the fact that Leslie was not as blasé as he let on, that he actually got off on his music heroes, Mick said he might have a surprise...

The night arrived and Leslie was elated when Mick, Charlie Watts and a few other stars' agents and managers came out of the living room.

It was a small, quaint get-together and I figured Charlie Watts was Mick's surprise. But Mick came over to me and said, "Answer the door with Leslie at midnight".

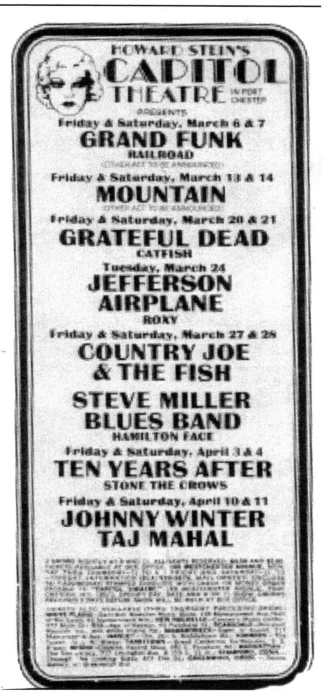

I was very curious, but patient, and when the doorbell rang at midnight, I grabbed Leslie - we opened the front door.

Standing there was John Lennon, decked out in his black Spanish Zorro outfit, whip and all. Flipping his whip - John yelled out in a Spanish accent: "Someone order a Rock & Roll hero."

It was a very dramatic entrance by a very dramatic man.

The party was just starting. Mr. Lennon proudly entered the quaint gathering with his then girlfriend May Pang. He approached me and whispered in my ear "thanks for singing at my session." (' Stand By Me')

It was quite a rush for all involved, especially Leslie. It was time to bring out the 'goodies'. In an effort to be discreet, Leslie nudged me towards the vanity room, the tiny bathroom in the entryway. I nudged Mick and he nudged John and John nudged May and the five of us found ourselves squeezing into this tiny vanity bathroom. Fortunately, Leslie West had at that time slimmed down to a mere 340 lbs.

Then John Lennon belted out: "Are we fuckin' crazy?" "Like, does anybody at this fuckin' party not know what we're doing?"

We were from the *Beatles*, the Stones and *Mountain* and we were trying to hide in this squeezebox.

It was quite ridiculous and after a huge laugh, we all fell out of the bathroom to an applauding group of managers toking on an enormous joint. As one of them blurted out: "Don't hide it - Divide it boys and girls."

# Thomas Edison's nuts

That's right, I am the proud owner of one of Mr. Edison's nuts - brass nuts, that is. The brass nuts he made by hand to be used in constructing one of the first generators ever built. This generator had it's home the Massachusetts Institute of Technology in Cambridge, near Boston, where it stood on display for years.

As it happened, MIT was the alma mater of our brilliant road-crew: Mike and Tom. When the college called upon them to help move the generator to the Washington Museum they snagged a few of the nuts with some other little things.

They gave me one of the nuts for the purpose of holding down my right high-hat. This effect would allow me to have a sock cymbal ride without having to use the cross-arm style made famous by Ringo Starr. Since then a drum accessory company developed a lock for the sock cymbal.

But I've still got Thomas Edison's brass nut!

# JethroTull
## and
## Mountain
### MAY 28, 1970
### 8:00 — 10:00 P.M.
### SELBY STADIUM
### $2.50
### RAIN OR SHINE

Me and Les at the Crystal Palace - London, England

## Timin' is everything

Hershey Pennsylvania was our umpteenth gig and I was feeling very confident about my position in *Mountain*. I decided to confront Felix and Leslie about a pay raise.

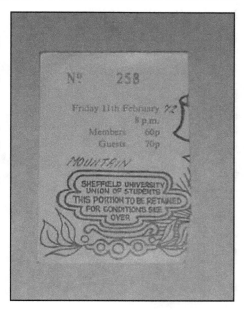

Unbeknownst to me however, Felix and Leslie were already having a private meeting about giving me a surprise raise. I knocked on the door and announced my request and succeeded in cutting in half what they originally had in mind.

I should have kept my mouth shut.

Hershey Pennsylvania, sweet deal gone bad. Timin' is Everything.

## Sink or Swim

When we arrived in England for our first tour, Felix didn't really know how *Mountain* was going to be received. *Cream* was still the reigning rock trio even though they had already disbanded. Felix was very anxious about the reception we would receive at our first gig, which was to be in the Crystal Palace. *Pink Floyd* was headlining.

Crystal Palace was set up with a beautiful pond in front of the stage. The audience sat beyond the pond on the surrounding lawn. When we began to play

there was, I would say, polite applause. We started really jamming but it was difficult to get a 'read' from the crowd because they were seated so far from the stage.

Felix turned around during "The Western" with that 'I don't know if they are diggin' it' look.

I screamed back at Felix: "Watch this!"

Without losing a beat, I tossed a stick off the cymbal and it jettisoned right into the middle of the pond. I could see some of the people in the crowd eye-balling the stick as it floated around in the middle of the drink. And sure enough, about a dozen people dove into the pond to retrieve it.

Felix gave me a great big smile and the crowd was on its feet.

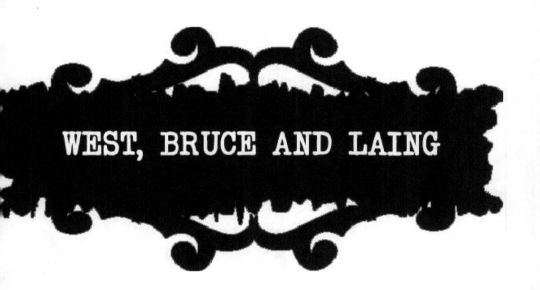

# WEST, BRUCE AND LAING

80th ANNIVERSARY SEASON

*Monday Evening, April 24, 1972, at 8:00 & 11:30*

**Ron Delsener presents**

# West, Bruce & Laing

# Probe – deathmobile

In the movie *Clockwork Orange* (1971), Stanley Kubrick used an 'Adams Probe 16' as the car driven by the villains around the English countryside while they were raping and pillaging everything in their path. The car was an experiment by the Adams Brothers. They wanted to produce the lowest sports car for the marketplace. Yes, lower than the Lotus. Each brother had one and it was quite the talk of the sports auto industry. Jimmy Webb (writer of McArthur Park, Wichita Lineman) bought one of the cars and Jack Bruce bought the other.

Flash forward to January 26, 1972. After an amazing recording session with Jack Bruce and Leslie West, we returned to Jack's mansion in the countryside for my birthday celebration. Please understand I'm still a young-buck in all this and if forming a band with Jack & Leslie wasn't the birthday present of all time, I don't know what is. Well, after being blown away musically, I was about to shit myself – Jack presented me with the Adams Probe as a birthday present. Have you ever been given a car for your birthday? Unfortunately, I couldn't hold down the multitude of drinks and celebration I had consumed and proceeded to throw up all over the car. Leslie laughed, "Now it's really yours." My wife Francy had her birthday a few weeks later. That night I was going to show off the car, and let me explain - this amazing piece of work was not more than sixteen inches high. You drove it lying down on your back. The rear view mirror was mounted on top of the windshield and you looked through the glass roof, which electrically recessed itself into the

back hood where the engine was sitting - right behind your head.

Later, when we picked up her birthday cake, a huge chocolate triple layer job from the Four Seasons no less, Francy carefully balanced the cake on her lap, trying not to stain her beautiful new birthday dress. And off we went, back to her party on Bayswater St. Then oops, here comes the rain as we were driving and oops the glass roof is in not responding. The battery light is on. Francy starts to freak as the drizzle turns into a full scale rain shower. No place to run, no place to park. Someone left the cake out in the rain. She tried to jettison the entire cake but, well you know, a very bad night indeed. Forget the cake, forget the dress, her hair was fucked and so was her birthday

# Corky Laing: A few rewards for a lot of hard travellin'

*Corky Laing behind the wheel of his Adam Brake II (remember, in Clockwork Orange?)*

party. Francy was not impressed with this car and never got in it again. Otherwise, upon our return to her party, everyone had a laugh, real good laugh.

A car like that would never make it through a day in Nantucket, where I was then living, with its cobblestone roads, salt air, etc. So at huge expense, I shipped the car back to Montreal. Of course, upon arrival in Montreal in April, there came a freak winter storm. There I was driving a 5-speed sports vehicle on the wrong side (English style), negotiating five inches of snow on the roads. The car looked buried – and once again the roof didn't work. Snow everywhere. Boy did I look cool.

Later that summer, the one time everything worked, Bob Mann from the Montreal Gazette saw me driving on St. Catherine Street. He stopped me and wrote an article for the newspaper. An engineering professor from McGill saw the article and called me to ask if I'd sell it. He had an idea of mounting a video viewer on the rear of the car and putting a screen in the console in order to monitor the rear view. For me the car was becoming an albatross, a real headache, so I agreed to everything. Recently I saw an ad for a new Acura complete with a rear view monitor – 30 years later! Who knew?

Melody Maker, January 24, 1972. Page 3

# Melody Maker

JANUARY 29, 1972    1s weekly    USA 30 cents

# JACK BRUCE IN MOUNTAIN

by CHRIS
CHARLESWORTH

## Paul adds a Wing

ARTHUR MacDUGGAN joins and the former Thunderclap Newman

JACK BRUCE: he's been playing with Leslie West and Corky Laing

JACK BRUCE may be joining "Mountain," the American rock group. After news that West will be the vocal, the guitarist and the group have decided that...

## Jazz invasion

A MAMMOTH gathering of Jazz stars has been slated up to play a festival in May in a concert organised by important Jazz buffs...

## What next for the guitar?

SEE PAGE 23

## Oldest Groupie

```
"Dust never sleeps"
                Neil Young
```

Our first European tour, I kept noticing this lovely old lady (I mean old!) hanging around the various stage doors in London, Paris & Brussels. She seemed nice enough and she had a lovely Scottish accent. I figured  maybe she was Jack's grandmother or great aunt. But when I brought her to Jack's attention, he had no idea who she was.

At one point, I approached her out of curiosity and she said that she was a big fan and especially loved Jack Bruce.  You want to sleep with Jack?" I asked "oh yes", she replied "I'd love to".

Well the good news was, at least she was a woman.

The bad news, she was 86 years old.

She was probably one of our feistiest groupies – at least when she wasn't sleeping.

# Fiction or non-fiction

Jack was amazing when it came down to industry "weasels'. He hated them all. Our Manager in England and Europe was Robert Stigwood and when *West, Bruce and Laing* headlined the Rainbow Theatre in London, Robert brought in a huge jar of caviar from Paris. It must have been worth a small fortune.

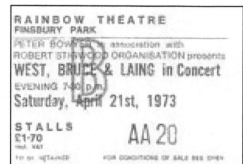

Jack accepted it gracefully on behalf of the group. He asked Leslie and I if we like caviar and after we shook our heads, he proceeded to toss the entire jar across the dressing room and smashed this most gracious gift against the wall. Well we didn' t have proper crackers to eat it with. Jack then insisted we proceed to the stage to play our music.

To this day I believe Jack thinks less of some of the industry people than he did of that jar of caviar.

*"I don't remember much about West, Bruce and Laing except that it was a great deal of fun."*

Jack Bruce, interview WNEW, 1977.

# Jack and the Italian army

There was never a dull moment with Jack Bruce. We'd all keep an eye out for him when we were in the public eye. In Rome a riot was about to erupt because Jack refused to play an encore.

The promoter, who resembled Marlon Brando in the Godfather, basically told the band, unless we performed the, encore, he would not guarantee our safety in Rome. We decided to play.

But Jack had to make sure everyone knew how pissed-off he was about being forced to play. As we walked down the path to the stage, lined on both sides for security by a hundred or so armed soldiers, Jack kept screaming: "You fuckin' spaghetti vendors."

He was trying to get a rise out of the armed men, but the soldiers just stared straight ahead at attention while he continued to shout.

Later, when trying to make our getaway, we discovered that they had shot the tyres out on the equipment truck and our limo.

We grabbed a cab and got the fuck out of Italy.

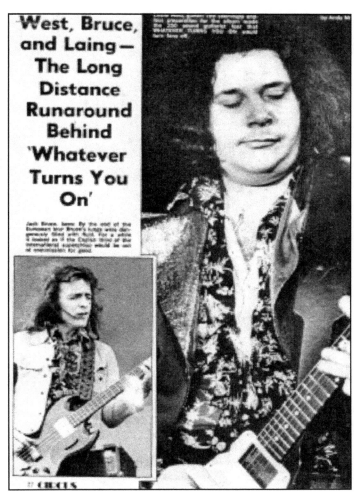

West, Bruce, and Laing — The Long Distance Runaround Behind 'Whatever Turns You On'

## Mini-castle mini-orgy

*West Bruce and Laing* was a beast. It was big, hairy, and scary loud. Jack was the mouth and the voice: with biting teeth, and a very loud bark and howl. Leslie was the guts: the dark soul, the weight, and the muscle. And if you ask anyone involved, I would probably have been the back end. There was no brain in the beast. It just moved around, pushing its way through Europe, England and the USA.

We bashed out records that were testosterone driven - only recording exactly what we felt at that given moment. This 'feeling' fluctuated depending on what medication was sniffing its way through the studios at the time. I do believe there were some very interesting moments on tape.

ı Copenhagen, *West, Bruce and Laing* was treated to an after-hours "orgy". It took place ɔmewhere in the hills at a mini-palace where the current royalty resided. Yeah, they were horny royalty who regularly entertained wealthy oriental investors and decadent Rock & .ollers. We all got pretty sloshed that night: the Orientals, the road crew and the band. .nd at some point in the evening, we all converged in the huge foyer, where a theatre was ɛt up.

Vhen the music started, some Euro-Disco shit, out came these three thespians (two ⁓omen and a man) acting out "fucking". There was about thirty of us watching this mini- ›rgy on stage.

ure enough, the crew started to get a little fidgety and our infamous 'hung like a race orses' road manager ("Mr. J. T.") decided to show-off his wears. Down he went to join ı. However, being in front of a crowd had its effect on him; the racehorse choked. And ɔ did the thespian who was trying to swallow the racehorse.

.fter that embarrassing performance by Mr. J. T., we decided to give him an advanced irthday present by treating him to the S & M room located down in the cellar of his mini- astle.

# West-Bruce-Laing

## DECEMBER 15, 1972 ONLY

# PARKING

ENTER FROM BROAD STREET ONLY AT PROGRESS PLACE
AND PROCEED TO PARKING LOT 5/6

## Spectrum

The set-up was as follows. You never see the female (hopefully) dominatrix. The beds were simple, raised wooden planks. You were tied down with your penis inserted through a hole in the plank. The dominatrix would then do her thing from underneath the plank-bed. So anyway, he was tied up and couldn't see who was doing what to him.

After five minutes in the cellar, we heard this wild scream and Mr. J. T. came running and screaming out of there.

Apparently she threatened to cut off his dick if he didn't co-operate. I never did understand the S & M thing.

One of the greatest advantages of being part of a successful ensemble (the beast) is that you can hide out in it. You sort of move along inside of the beast as the beast moves around the world.

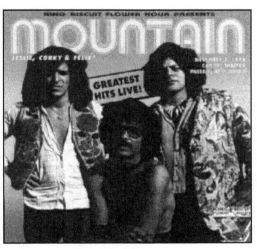

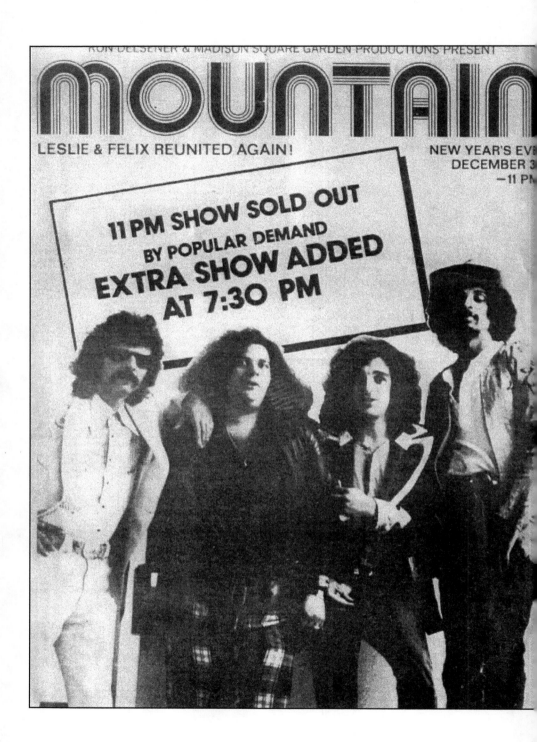

# The nose knows

I would not consider this a "drug-war-story" but there was a time late in the game where Felix was not being as careful as he should when it came to sniffin' stuff. In Athens Ohio 1974, someone offered him a package of white powder and Felix just whoofed it up his nose. Leslie and I were a little shocked: first of all he didn't know exactly what it was, secondly he didn't even offer to share it.

Anyway, an hour later, we were on stage and I looked at Felix playing away and to my amazement there was a huge glossy snot hanging about three inches out of his nostrils.

He didn't feel it or even see it. He just kept on grooving away, eyes closed. I just about fell off my stool, I was laughing so hard. Everyone in the front rows of the audience was laughing at him as well. I hit Leslie with a drumstick to get his attention. When Leslie caught a glimpse of this huge (four inches at this point) snot, he just about fell down. It was too fuckin' much!

Felix, oblivious to all this, actually got really pissed when the song began to fall apart. In between belly laughs, I pointed to his nose and he flipped when he looked down at it. I mean he literally flipped - he flipped his head around to try and get rid of it. Instead, the snot wound all the way around his head and smacked him in the eye on the other side of his face. This must have burned like hell as he immediately tried to wipe it away - without stopping his bass playing.

The audience in the front was hysterical. We eventually stopped the song and Felix apologized saying he had a cold, which led to this runny nose...

**Mr Peter Frampton. An amazing singer, songwriter and guitarist.**

**Michael, Donny and Calvin Johnson rehearsing in VFW Hall, Nantucket, Mass. Winter 1976.**

With Dickie Betts

# On my way to Georgia

In the summer of 1975 I needed a cooling–off period. I left the *Leslie West Band* and retreated to Nantucket to write songs. There was a seven-piece band out of Boston called the *Johnson Brothers* that would play regularly at the "Chicken Box" in Nantucket. I hired them to help me demo the new songs I had written. (Some were co-written with a good friend and popular novelist Frank Conroy). We worked through the winter of 1976 and eventually brought the record Plant Studio truck over to Nantucket to record seven of the tunes.

Next was the beginning. I sent these tapes to a wonderful human being in New York, Ron Delesner, who directed me to another amazing human being, John Eastman, who, within days had arranged a solo record deal with Steve Wax at Elektra Asylum Records. I was blown away. I had just wanted to write music, but now had a record deal with the hottest label in the world. Taking a cash advance, I set off to Macon Georgia, home of *Otis Redding*, the *Allman Brothers* and some of the best southern bands in the business. I was the first Northern rocker to record at Capricorn Studios at Macon, Georgia, and - for some reason - they treated me like a king,

The *Johnson Brothers* didn't last long in Macon, but said the whole experience ultimately was the best lesson in  the music business that they ever had. Over the next decade, they were to produce *New Kids on the Block*, *New Edition* and *Peter Wolf* (with Mick Jagger) - selling millions of albums  combined.

Now I had to make the record: "Makin' it On the Street." I was fortunate to have the opportunity to record with some great session musicians as well as an old acquaintance Eric Clapton and Dicky Betts. Charlie Daniels, Neal Larson and Bonnie Bramlett also joined in for some nightly jamming.

We had a hell of an autumn, but it was now time to go and mix the record in LA.   One night, Greg Allman popped over to Beverly Wiltshire

Hotel to escape his domestic bliss. After lengthy discussions about Capricorn Records and the Macon, Georgia soap operas, we finally crashed out.

Little did I realise we were in a bed together and in the morning he rolled over thinking I was Cher and was about to give me a great big southern morning hug. I sobered up real quick enough to jump the hell outta bed before it looked like I was switching teams.

The phone rang, and when I picked up to answer, I was hit by a barrage of locker-room language Lenny Bruce would have found offensive. It was Cher and she wanted to know who the fuck Greg was sleeping with. I introduced myself and confessed he had slept with me.

"I knew it," she cried. "I pushed him too far."

I had to interrupt her to tell her that nothing happened. She kept on apologizing for kicking him outta the house. It was way too much information for me. Everything smoothed out and lent Greg six bucks to get his corvette out of the garage so he could return to his Domestic Bliss. And as much as I love Greg Allman, I'll never switch teams.

You gotta love LA.

E-45393-A
(SP)
ASCAP
Youngbuck
Publishing
Intro: :14
Time: 2:58
Close-Fade
℗ 1977 by
Elektra
Records
FOR RADIO
STATION
USE ONLY
MONO

**CORKY LAING**
**SEE ME THROUGH**
(C. Laing & F. Conroy)
Produced by John Sandlin for
Youngbuck Productions Inc.
From The Album
"Makin' It On The Street"

® elektra

Mfg. by Elektra / Asylum / Nonesuch Records, 962 N. La Cienega Blvd., Los Angeles, Calif. 90069 / A Division of Warner Communications Inc.

## Salvador Dali

While preparing for my second solo record, I found myself swept up in the wildness that was Studio 54. You see I was waiting at the St. Regis Hotel for the president of the record label, and it was just up the block from the famous 'Den of Iniquity.' I would love to crack you up with Studio 54 stories but the only thing I remember is once watching three waiters banging two waitresses. That's it. I was living at the time on the record label's ticket and it is all a blur.

Returning one morning to the St. Regis, I had a couple of messages waiting for me at the front desk. One message was from my mother Sarah telling me she was arriving that day. The other message was an invitation to a party that night in Salvador Dali's suites. Salvador Dali? There must be some mistake.

As I turned to the concierge to ask about this Dali invite, my Mom came flying through the revolving door and greeted me with a great hug. She checked herself in at the St Regis, also at the label's expense. I had been waiting a week now and still no president. Good thing this was still the 'credit card and champagne golden years of Rock & Roll' (the likes of which will probably never be seen again). I was so glad to have had a pulse in order to enjoy those years.

Anyway, this Salvador Dali deal was curious and Sarah just flipped when I told her about the message. I tried to bring her down a few decibels by explaining it must be a mistake - but to no avail.

"You are so humble sometimes", she said, "but I'd love to meet Sal."

OK, OK, OK - we called to accept this mistaken invitation. Strangely though, we were then asked if we would like to swing by right away as well. When entering the hallway of his suite, I was totally mesmerised by the two women holding him up as he slowly made his way down the hall to ultimately give me a big hug.

"You are still so beautiful", he said to me. And he looked at Sarah and said: "Isn't he a beautiful boy". Sarah was stunned. "Of course he's beautiful, he's my son".

"Oh yes," Salvador confirmed in his exquisite Spanish accent, "it's so wonderful to see you in New York again, you must join us immediately, We go, we go." And the five of us shuffled off down the hall, out into the red carpeted steps and into the street to his waiting limousine.

The whole time, I couldn't help staring at one of his companions. She was probably the most beautiful woman I had ever seen. The fact that Salvador was totally confused about me... well, who cares. It didn't bother me if it didn't bother him. As we sat in the Limo, Salvador was silent. I thought he was staring at my crotch from behind his sunglasses. In those days, I wore all my pants like they were painted on in order to catch the female eyes – not his. Meanwhile, I couldn't take my eyes off his beautiful companion who had still not been introduced to us. Finally she took Sarah's hand and my hand and introduced herself as Stephanie (very Spanish). It turned out we were going to the Guggenheim Museum.

When we arrived we climbed an oval, ascending walkway til we reached a hologram. Salvador was just coming to check the layout of this one piece of art. Little did we all realise at the time, the public would later be lining up for blocks in order to see this one exhibit.

Stephanie, I found out, was Salvador's student. And at the museum she started doing business with the curator. Salvador took the opportunity to whisper in my ear. "My son, I would like to postpone tonight's get together until tomorrow. I've got something to attend to." I asked if I could attend to Stephanie and he smiled. "All in good time," and gave me a hug.

Sarah and I used his limo to get back to the St. Regis. She was thrilled. It was quite a story to tell her friends back home. Salvador F__ing Dali. She finally asked me how I met Salvador and why I had never told her anything about this friendship. I couldn't burst her bubble and whispered, "I'll explain later – all in good time."

To this day, I have no idea why Dali felt he knew me. Maybe he was just coming on to me. The party was never to be. But there was an address in South of Spain left on my message box, signed S. The president of the record company arrived a week later and we were off to another lifetime.

89

# Stickin' with the Happy Hooker

After nearly seven years of touring, first with *Mountain* and then *West Bruce and Laing*, I thought I'd take a short break from Leslie. (The Chicago Tribune called it "Corky Laing's Seven Year Bitch!") Nothing against Lester, we both had acquired some demons we had to sort out, if you get my drift.

During this down time, my lawyer asked me if I'd be interested in producing a single. I would have to write the song and it would have to be about SEX.

First question back to him: "Who's the artist?"

"Well," he said, "you'd have to stretch the artist-thing to, let's say, performer."

"OK weasel", I responded, "Who's the performer?"

"Well", he said, "She's not necessarily a musical performer..."

I interrupted jokingly, "So she's a sexual performer?"

"Who told you?" he replied.

"You can't be serious, a hooker, stripper, call-girl, lap-dancer?"

"Yep", he said, "all of these... It's Xaviera Hollander."

I had to sit down and get this figured out.

Xaviera Hollander had skipped the U.S. because of a very heavy scandal involving the New York Police Department. I forget the name of the scandal, but she was residing in Toronto temporarily while she filed for a residence permit in Canada. However, she could not use 'Hooker' as an occupation for this permit, so she put down 'Recording Artist'. And that's where I came in. She urgently needed to record some music before they threw her sorry, but well-rounded ass, out of Canada. He gave me a big check, and I was off to see what other pleasures were in store for me.

Upon my arrival at her Toronto apartment and after a few knocks, a soft sexy uropean voice called out to "come on in."

s I approached the back room, there she was, legs spread on the sofa, big welcoming smile. it down and join us", she whispered. "Us?" I replied and as I turned around there was my loody girlfriend from years passed "Marilyn Chambers." Marilyn? Xaviera? Marilyn? aviera? - Ohh-ohh. Well, this could be interesting.

a an effort to maintain my cool I took out my cassette player and suggested we get started.

Ok," Xaviera said and took her fingers and placed them right *there* and began a high-octane assage. Marilyn started to mount Xaviera with her back to me.

Whoa," I interrupted, "music! Music ladies" (mind you I don't know any drummer, let alone

ay musician who can't et into some lesbo ction.) Ultimately, the ession went very well xcept for one problem. he just would not stop laying with herself the whole time I was there. ven Marilyn got fed up ad left.

he song never did get eleased but Xaviera did. he was thrown out of anada that summer.

think she has a bed and reakfast in Denmark ow. Mick Jones, who elped me write the song, ent on to put a band agether called *Foreigner*. ut I don't think it was amed after Xaviera.

Murray couldn't believe his luck, who knew Madame K would accept his 2 for 1 pizza coupons at par.

MARYLYN v XAVIERA

91

BEST PART OF A MAN     L. Laing

Thinkin' 'bout love
Thinkin' 'bout pleasure
When a man and woman
Get it on together

There is no greater thrill
And don't we all know it
The only frustration
Is when we can't show it

Chorus

I know the best part of livin'
Is loving a man
The best part of a man
Is the one thing I'm gonna love
And just so I know
That the best part is real
I'm gonna take my man and love him
And that's all I'm gonna feel

Lovin's like music
With it's highs and lows
Every lover's a song
There ain't one I don't know

It's the past now
I got a new melody
It's the heart of something
The lovin' part of me

Repeat Chorus

# Kinky Mix'd up years

```
           Was it Cinderella,
           Who told Rockefella,
       That time is the Money of Love?

                   Kinky Friedrnan
```

During the 1980's at the Lone Star Cafe, New York, I met music performer and writer Kinky Friedman. Kinky was the leader of a Texas based, Country-Rock-Folked up-Bar Mitzvah band called *Kinky and the Texas Jew Boys*. Upon joining his band, he nicknamed me "Jewish Radar" because I picked up the tunes so quick.

I have to admit these were emotionally dark days for me. But then many of us hated ourselves in this decade. We could not look at ourselves in our mirrors, so we took them off the wall and snorted half of Peru's Gross National Product every New York minute for days upon days. It was like one long hangover.

Now let's rewind. Kinky was asked by Don Imus, a New York celebrity radio personality/ writer, to be the music composer for a Broadway show based on Don's critically acclaimed book "God's Other Son." The show was being presented to investors with the hope that it would make it to the Broadway stage. Since Don was a very generous person, we would all be promised a piece of the action upon its success.

Kinky gathered together some immense talent including Ratzo Sloman, Larry Campbel (guitarist for Bob Dylan) and booked first division recording facilities like the Record Plant in New York. Little did we know that Don was himself going through a very "Dark Period," struggling with some of his own vices. Since I was one of the project producers, Don would give me the payroll to disburse responsibly to the players. One night, when he ran a close second to being dead, he handed me an envelope that was supposed to contain $1500 for the band.

I trusted Don and stuffed the envelope in my jacket and waited till I got back home to do the payroll. To my amazement, there wasn't $1500 in the envelope, there $15,000. That's right - fifteen thousand dollar bills. I said to myself: "Wow, a $13,500 tip. Imus is a fuckin' generous guy." Then I thought about it - no way. When I returned the $13,500, it blew Imus away. He couldn't believe anyone, especially a Rock & Roll drummer would be that honest and respectful.

Respect was the buzzword. Don is a class act, but it seems he has, in his lifetime, fallen off the wagon a few times. I happened to bare witness to one of the worst falls.

**The " Kinkster.'**

It happened after a very productive session at the Record Plant. I walked into the bathroom to take a leak when I came upon this immense body lying on the bathroom floor, pants down

Now that Montreal Expos pitcher **Bill Lee** has made his mark in rock & roll — on the recent **Warren Zevon** album, *Bad Luck Streak in Dancing School*, which includes a track bearing his name — "the Spaceman," as he is fondly known to fans, is moving on to movies. Lee will be one of several ballplayers featured in an upcoming documentary called *I Lost the Grounder in the Sun*, which is being scored by ex-**Mountain** drummer **Corky Laing** and his latest band, the **Mix**.

Although the colorful lefty was fined by baseball commissioner Bowie Kuhn last year after remarking that he liked to season his morning pancakes with marijuana, Lee insists he is not a nut. "Listen," he says, "the brain is divided into two halves, left and right. The left half controls the right side of your body and the right half your left side. Therefore, left-handers are the only people in their right minds."

(with toilet paper sticking to something), and snoring. It was my millionaire DJ friend having a casual nap. I guess the nap took hold before he had a chance to finish dropping-a-Nixon. It's not a pretty sight to see a millionaire crashed out on a bathroom floor. In fact, he landed in the same position as Steve Tyler had ten years before, on that exact same floor. This experience is one that all of us, who are rehab degenerates, must flash on before we decide to dive into another drug infested situation.

It's a reminder that the floor is there to stop anyone of us who want to go too far.

**With Vidas Gerilitus**

The Mix, early 1980s.

Stu Daye, Chris
Meridith and
David Graham.

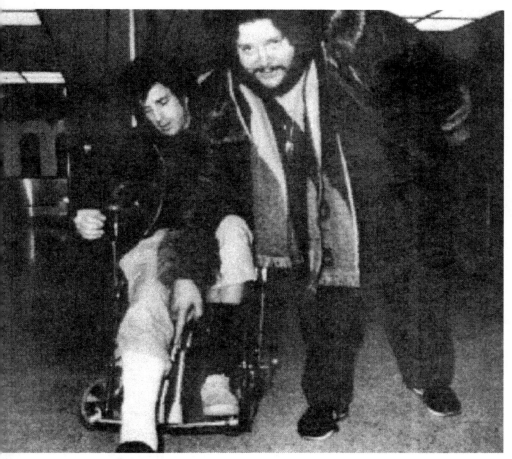

**Leslie giving me a hand with my leg. Also in the early 1980s.**

## Break a leg

I've always hated that saying: 'Break a Leg.' It is, of course, supposed to bring good luck to a performer as he hits the stage. But it was exactly what I did at a club (Hell's Angels' Hangout) in Heywood, California, February 1981. Instead of coming around the drum set to take my bow, I had to be the big showman and jump over the top of the kit. My head smashed against some hanging lights (I didn't see it coming), and boy, did I hit that stage for the finale.

The audience was stunned when they saw this amazing landing. As I heard my ankle crunch, I saw my drumming career vanish into the California night air. They dragged me off stage to a chorus of Oooo's and Ahhhh's then rushed me to the nearest hospital. To make matters worse,

I flat out refused to be operated on by the doctor on call that night. He had just been called in from a big party and was as drunk as a skunk. Instead they hit me up with every bit of morphine in Haywood and threw me on the first flight back east.

Surprisingly, those were the most creative months I can remember. I had to learn to play with my left foot on the right bass drum. I played sort of left-handed (or is that left-footed?). Kinky called me the Special Olympics drummer. As I later found out, Levon Helm had a broken leg when he recorded 'Big Pink'.

It's a scary life if you' re missing a piece of yourself.

# Rock Star's Wife Gets Up to 4 Years In Gunshot Death

# Rock A... Shot De... Wife He...

## Wife Convicted in Slaying

## Tampering in Pappalardi Case

## Grieving girlfriend tells of last hours w

# 'I SENT MY ROC
# LOVER
# TO HIS

Felix
Pappalardi
in his
heyday
during the
Sixties,
when he
was a
guiding
light for
groups like
Cream.

By M
THE
rock
lardi
abou
home
week

The
helpe
psych
'60s,
to die
Colli
East
Sund

"I
I new
said
Valle

# THE BEST OF TIMES

**Felix fishing in Nantucket Island.**

# THE WORST OF TIMES

ain musician

## STAR HOME DEATH'

**VALERIE: Mistress told Pappalardi to forget her and return to his wife.**

ATRICK
of slain
Pappa-
esterday
er lover
h after a

ar, who
the
d of the
ly shot
fe, Gail
plush
artment

eve I'll
again,"
mposer
27, who

dated Pappalardi for a
year.

"I told him 'If you love
me, leave me. Go home
to your wife,' " said a
weeping Miss Merians,
'she's suffered
enough.' "

He did — and a few
hours later he was dead.

Miss Merians said she
met Pappalardi at a
rock club last May and
that his wife found out
about them early on.

"Gail was very aware
of me," said Miss
Merians.

"Felix and I were

deeply in love and he
wanted to marry me."

One day, Miss Merians
said she called Pappa-
lardi's wife to confess.

"I told her 'I'm in love
with your husband,' "
she said. "I told her we
were having an affair."

Miss Merians said
Pappalardi was enraged
that she hurt his wife
and they broke up.

But, she added, he
missed her and resumed
the affair after a two-
week separation.

Pappalardi was at her
Upper East Side apart-
ment Friday when they
fought and she sent him
home to his wife.

"He was the most won-
derful human being I've
ever met," she said. "He
would have walked
through fire for me.

"I love him so much,"
she said. "I just wish I
could bring him back."

waited for police.

Miss Collins, who co-
wrote the group Cream's
hit songs "Strange
Brew" and "World of
Pain" with Pappalardi,
led police to the bedroom
where his body lay.

Pappalardi, who was
medically deaf from his
years as a bass guitarist
with the popular late '60s
group Mountain, was
lying in bed with a bullet
wound in the neck.

Police recovered the
alleged murder weapon,
a .38-caliber Derringer,
as well as a .38 revolver.
Both were unlicensed.

Miss Collins' lawyer,
Hal Meyerson, said the
shooting was "definite-
ly" a mistake.

Miss Collins, who has
been with Pappalardi for
20 years since his Green-
wich Village folk music
days, was taken to Belle-

# The murder

Felix and Gail had plenty of free time in Nantucket, probably way too much free time. I call that kind of time "anti-time" because, unless you get something going, it's going to come back against you.

During the late 1970's, Felix and Gail's behaviour became pretty erratic. He shipped his antique twelve-cylinder Rolls Royce (which had once belonged to Hermann Goring) from a storage garage in New York City to Nantucket. He also shipped over another of his antique "Boat-Back" Rolls, one that was so beautiful it could have belonged to the Queen of England. But Nantucket is just not the place for such things - the salt air, the sand everywhere, the harsh winters, not to mention roads that resemble horse trails and the cobblestone driveways. Cars don't last long there. On top of that, Nantucket is not the place to be pretentious. You don't show anything off, let alone antique luxury cars.

There was many a night I was invited to drive the back roads of Nantucket while Felix used the resisters up on the hydro poles for target practice with his magnum and automatic rifle. (Felix manipulated the gun permit laws by making friends with a few influential people in Nantucket.) I stopped playing cowboys and Indians with Felix when I discovered bullet shells in the bedroom walls of his cottage. My wife and I would carefully frisk Felix and Gail when they came over for a visit: the last thing we wanted was a shoot out at the "Corky Corral." Our horses would freak out.

Apart from his amazing musical skills, Felix was a very intelligent human being - that is, when he wasn't under the spell of Gail Collins. It was unfortunate, but Gail would keep him from his family and friends by not letting him know that they were trying to get in contact with him. Felix wasn't cognizant. I'm sure he had an idea she was covering for him, but doubt he knew to what extent she was deceiving him. As a result, theirs was a very intense relationship, a very dependent relationship, and a very sordid relationship.

Again, guns were everywhere and drugs (prescription and non-prescription) were always on display. And their attitudes were very manic. One day they were up, the next day they were depressed. Gail had a wicked laugh (and I mean wicked!) that would scare the shit out of anyone. She was, in my opinion, just plain scary. To this day, I cannot for the life of me understand why Felix would buy her a gun unless he had a death wish.

There were times earlier that year when Felix would be hours late for a session. Once he came in with twenty stitches in his head and said a pan in the kitchen fell on his head. I remember they kept their pans in the bottom cupboards. He would have to be crawling on the kitchen floor to have had anything fall on him, let alone rip open his face. Can you imagine living that way? Well maybe he imagined another life and when he decided to finally leave her, she took out that gift and basically

"Sam Cooke'd" him. Jealousy? Intoxication? Psycho? As Leslie West once said, the moral of this morbid story is: never, ever, buy your wife a gun.

Till this day, I agree with Felix's family who stand by the notion that Gail would have killed him "gun or no gun". It was just the easiest way, to pull the trigger. But then again everything was just a bit too easy; there was too much leisure time - 'anti-time'. And it'll come back and get you. Gail got Felix. This is one of the only murders on record though the courts called it negligent homicide. Negligent? Felix may have been the negligent one. He had no business giving her the gun.

A year earlier, Felix and I were in San Diego and he purchased a ceramic sculpture of two old men fishing. He said he would send it to me in Nantucket because, after a couple of decades on the road together, he finally considered me a good friend. He said that's what he wanted us to look like at 80: two old farts fishin'. I never did receive the gift but I remember that moment like it was a moment ago.

Felix and I had become great friends and I'm sorry we never got to be two old farts fishin'.

1970: Felix in the moment

The best part of being a drummer is making your bass player proud

Corky Laing
at the
Nurembürg Rock Festiva

Dirk (road manager), Rudolph Schenker (jammer) and Cozy Powell's red drum set

# The biggest cowbell

In 1986, Mountain released "Go for Your Life" and we were immediately invited to join Deep Purple for their European Tour. All the same, we had to pay $5000 per show, or something like that. You had to pay to play. It took this tour for me to find out just how low people in this business could go. After our dues were paid we really had no money left over for production effects.

Leslie had an idea. The only thing the European audience might recognize is a cowbell. "Why don't you call LP (a percussion manufacturer) and see if they'll make you a large cowbell."

I had no idea how happy LP was to hear from me. They claimed they sold more cowbells

107

in 1970 after the release of our album than they could manufacture. "OK," I said. "Since you never compensated me then, how about doing something for me now."

"Whatever you want, Corky."

"Well, I'll tell you what I want. I want the biggest cowbell ever made: seven or eight feet high; 4 or 5 feet wide, OK?" "OK," they said.

I got a call the next week from them telling me that the biggest cowbell ever made was ready. I hustled down to LP headquarters and there it was, a massive, black, heavy, tin cowbell. Now how on earth do we transport this thing, I wondered?

Thousands of dollars later, *Mountain* was in Europe, playing to concerts of 100,000 people. But every time we rolled this black thing on stage for the big finally, instead of a mar of applause, we got this puzzled silence. What the fuck is that? "Did a Stealth Bomber crash?" "Did they borrow the Monolith from *Space Odyssey 2001*?" "Where are the fuckin' monkeys?" To our dismay, it wasn't working.

Fortunately, Ritchie Blackmore, who caught our show a few times, noticed that cowbells aren't black in Europe; they are gold. That night we found all the gold paint we could and coated the sucker. From then on, every time the cowbell was rolled out on stage, the crowd went crazy.

Thank you Ritchie.

After the tour was over, we had to figure out how to get this enormous cowbell back to LP. That was their only request. Well we didn't. It's still sitting at Henny's Rehearsal, in London England, for anyone who cares. Hurry up and wait.

| ARRIVAL TIMES | | | | |
|---|---|---|---|---|
| GROUP | DATE | TIME / FROM | PICK-UP | TOUR MANAGER |
| Deep Purple | July 3rd | Airport Munich, 3.5o pm from Madrid by LH 169 | Limo | Ossi Hoppe/ Joe Baribeault |
| | July 4th | see above | | |
| Meat Loaf | July 5th | Band: Airport Nürnberg, 1o.35 pm from London by LH o59 | Bus | Udo Schaar |
| | July 5th | Meat Loaf: pick-up in Munich t.b.a. | Car | Udo Schaar |
| Roger Chapman & The Shortlist | July 5th | Airport Nürnberg, 2.o5 pm from London via Frankfurt by LH 881 | Bus | Rainer Lindner |
| Mountain | July 4th | Airport Frankfurt, 3.4o pm from Madrid by LH 161 | Bus | Michael Gehrke |
| Rodgau Monotones | July 5th | Crest Hotel Nürnberg by car | | Roland Fackel |

The agenda for the Europe tour.

**Jesse Ventura at the top of the mountain (Excalibur story)**

# Jesse "The Body" Ventura

Leslie came up with a brilliant storyline idea for our "Hard Times" promo video. He thought of doing a variation of the "Excalibur" story - the sword in the stone. But of course we would replace the sword with a guitar.

We tried getting Andre the Giant to play the heavy who, even with all his strength, could not remove the guitar embedded in the rock. Then, as our storyline had it, Leslie was to excuse Andre and pull the guitar out of the rock himself.

Well Andre refused to be the one who could not successfully pull the guitar out. He was, after all the wrestling champ of the world.

Leslie and I loved the idea though and were determined to find another wrestler.

Enter Jesse Ventura, a Vietnam vet who was more than happy to be in a Rock video with *Mountain.*

The band always had an underlying allegiance with the Vietnam Vets, especially owing to songs like: "Flowers of Evil".

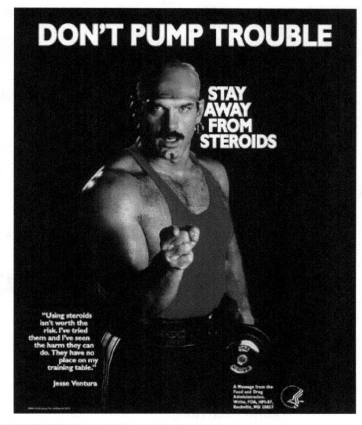

Later when shooting the video, I was curious why Jesse didn't also feel this role to be a betrayal to his power-profile.

He said he had a bigger agenda on his mind and Leslie should be the one to win the battle with gravity. Little did we know then he would later become Governor Ventura.

Two of the greatest living music industry people: Dick Clark and Bob Ansell

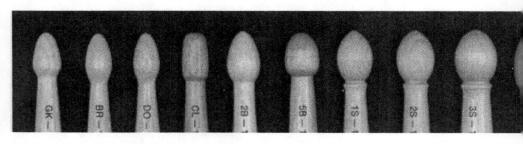

**ABOVE AND OPPOSITE: Sticking with some great company.**

# Promotion in motion

After decades on the road, you think you've seen and done just about every decadent thing. And you feel you've done everything possible to promote your music. Well yeah... I thought so until Leslie and I went on the Howard Stern Radio show in the mid 1990's. Howard was, and is (I hope) a Leslie West fan and loved the words to "Yasgur's Farm", a lyric I am very proud to have written. It describes what I believe was the essence of the 1960's...very vague.

*"Look at me,*
*I believe it's true,*
*You're a part of me,*
*I'm a part of you."*

In order to promote a benefit gig along with K-Rock, we were invited to Howard's morning show. I thought promotion was the agenda. It was, for about thirty seconds until Les started discussing his sex life and how he keeps his penis erect by shooting it up with his special (legal) medication. For some reason, Howard kept the discussion alive instead of pressing the panic button. I guess he was curious. Now, I've known Les for about thirty years, but this was the first time he had gone this far on this particular subject. For about twenty minutes, he described how to insert a needle into the head of your penis and inject the liquid, which stimulates the muscles and keeps the penis erect - hard as a rock for about four hours. The sensitivity factor is not compromised whatsoever and you, in fact, ejaculate during that erect period. All this information on our promotion time.

For the first time in my life (let alone on a radio show) I had absolutely nothing to say. Howard seemed mesmerized by the interview. I don't think we sold 'record one' but I'm sure, as a result of Leslie's dick promotion, there are a lot of firm ones walking around New York. So much for serious promotion. A firm dick can do a lot more for your career when you live to talk about it.

**Keeping good company with Buddy Rich and Gene Krupa**

| MODEL | HICKORY WOOD TIP | HICKORY NYLOWOOD | DENSIWOOD WOOD TIP | DENSI-NYLOWOOD |
|---|---|---|---|---|
| PARADE AND DRUM COR | 35 | | 35 | |
| | 25 | | .250 | |
| | 15 | | .SD | |
| BIG OLIDE | 5B | 5BN | 5BD | 5BE |
| MASKELL HASJR | 2B | 2BN | 2BD | 2BE |
| CORKY LAING | CL | CLN | CLD | CLE |
| DONNY OSBORNE | DO | DON | DOD | DOE |
| BUDDY RICH | BR | BRN | BRD | BRE |
| GENE KRUPA | GK | GKN | GKD | GKE |
| JAKE HANNA | 21A | 21N | 21D | 21E |
| BARRET DEEMS | 19A | 19N | 19D | 19E |
| DANNY D'IMPERIO | 18A | 18N | 18D | 18E |
| DANNY SERAPHINE | 8A | 8N | 8D | 8E |
| BOB ROS-ENGARDEN | 7A | 7N | 7D | 7E |
| OLLIE BROWN | 6A | 6N | 6D | 6E |
| PETER ERSKINE | 5A | 5N | 5D | 5E |
| BEV BEVAN | 4A | | 4D | |
| NIGEL OLSSON | 3A | 3N | 3D | 3E |
| DENNIS ST. JOHN | 2A | 2N | 2D | 2E |
| STUDENT | 1A | 1N | 1D | 1E |

## The music don't care

When you have a gentleman like Levon Helm that you can call a friend you are one of the blessed humans on this planet.

One summer afternoon, Levon, Sandy, and I were having a lovely chat at his home (a wonderfully constructed barn, which is in fact a number of different barn designs constructed into one) and the concept of music sampling, electronic sequencing, and quantizing came up. Since he is, and always will be, one of my greatest music inspirations, I was digging deep to suss out his 'take' on these subjects, and his general impression of the digital-music world especially from a drummer's point of view.

At some point in the conversation, as we were both quite casually glowing, he lifted his head slowly, deep in thought, and in a very rich southern drawl, he calmly whispered: "Corky, music is very special.  You can do anything to music – music don't care!"

Playing with Meatloaf was at the very least an interesting gig. Since I was the only other golfer in the band, he would invite me along to play while he improved his golf swing. Off the course, I was improving my musicianship with the challenging and often cryptic drum arrangements written by John Steinman. To this day I believe Jim has it in for drummers.

# Cork

Throughout my music career as a player, I also had the opportunity to live and breathe on the other side of the music business. It was cold. A few years as an executive at Chappell Music Publishing and a few at Polygram Records gave me this new perspective. I was amazed to discover the contempt many of those business types in the music industry have for the artists they are supposed to represent.

It is not a healthy environment to play in. I found that if an artist wants to succeed, he must be very astute, and very lucky. I know, it sounds like a cliché but it is up to the artist to rise above the bullshit and enjoy the muse while it lasts.

I am also sorry to say some of my best friends and peers could not rise above it and crashed while trying. I dedicate this book to them and their courageous efforts to make brilliant music while they ascended in their career – especially the drummers. The ones that could not "Stick It", but stick to it: Keith Moon, John Bonham, Bobby Chinard and so many more including Cozy Powell and of course Levon Helm.

**Acoustic Jam with James Taylor and George R.**

**Eric Schenkman, guitarist with Cork**

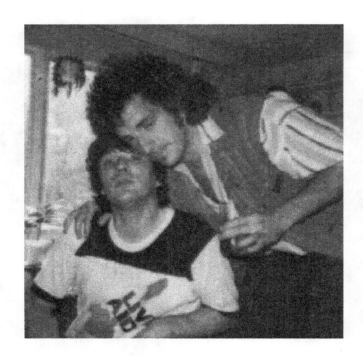

**Rick Danko**

**Richard Manuel**

**The boys from *The Band***

**Great Inspiration**
**Dr John**

**Great motivation**
**Don Henley**

**Great perspiration
Iggy Pop with Junior**

"These were my bed time stories. It's no wonder I haven't slept in fourteen years".
Colin Laing

After all these years, one would think the magic is over - it was left by the roadside somewhere outside Armpit, Nebraska.

On the contrary, I have had the opportunity these past years to hook up with Eric Schenkman in Toronto. We write, record and perform under the name Cork. At this time, we are finishing off our second CD, recorded in Cork, Ireland with Noel Redding on bass.

Nothing has changed. I still feel totally overwhelmed with enthusiasm. The magic, the muse and the music are still in the air, in the water and very much in my life. Life is good and to quote a good friend: "everything turns out right when NOW comes around." (Tukaz)

**Corky Laing**

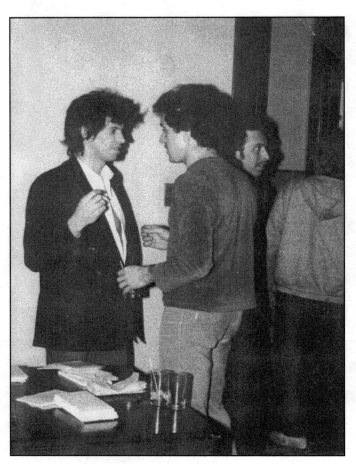

**A medical consultation**

# GONZO
## Books

There is still such a thing as alternative Publishing

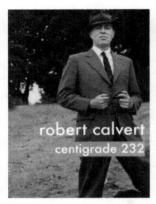

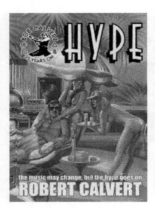

Robert Newton Calvert: Born 9 March 1945, Died 14 August 1988 after suffering a heart attack. Contributed poetry, lyrics and vocals to legendary space rock band Hawkwind intermittently on five of their most critically acclaimed albums, including Space Ritual (1973), Quark, Strangeness & Charm (1977) and Hawklords (1978). He also recorded a number of solo albums in the mid 1970s. CENTIGRADE 232 was Robert Calvert's first collection of poems.

Hype    'And now, for all you speed ing street smarties out there, the one you've all been waiting for, the one that'll pierce your laid back ears, decoke your sinuses, cut clean thru the schlock rock, MOR/crossover, techno flash mind mush. It's the new Number One with a bullet … with a bullet … It's Tom, Supernova, Mahler with a pan galac tic biggie …' And the Hype goes on. And on. Hype, an amphetamine hit of a story by Hawkwind collaborator Robert Calvert. Who's been there and made it back again. The debriefing session starts here.

Rick Wakeman is the world's most unusual rock star, a genius who has pushed back the barriers of electronic rock. He has had some of the world's top orchestras perform his music, has owned eight Rolls Royces at one time, and has broken all the rules of com posing and horrified his tutors at the Royal College of Music. Yet he has delighted his millions of fans. This frank book, authorised by Wakeman himself, tells the moving tale of his larger than life career.

"So many books, so little time."
Frank Zappa

There are nine Henrys, pur
ported to be the world's
first cloned cartoon charac
ter. They live in a strange
lo fi domestic surrealist
world peopled by talking
rock buns and elephants on
wobbly stilts.

They mooch around in their
minimalist universe suffer
ing from an existential
crisis with some genetically
modified humour thrown in.

Marty Wilde on Terry Dene: "Whatever
happened to Terry becomes a great deal
more comprehensible as you read of the
callous way in which he was treated by
people who should have known better
many of whom, frankly, will never know
better    of the sad little shadows of
the past who eased themselves into
Terry's life, took everything they
could get and, when it seemed that all
was lost, quietly left him — Dan Wood
ing's book tells it all."

Rick Wakeman: "There have
always been certain 'careers'
that have fascinated the
public, newspapers, and the
media in general. Such
include musicians, actors,
sportsmen, police, and not
surprisingly, the people who
give the police their employ
ment: The criminal. For the
man in the street, all these
careers have one thing in
common: they are seemingly
beyond both his reach and,
in many cases, understanding
and as such, his only associ
ation can be through the
media of newspapers or tele
vision. The police, however,
will always require the ser
vices of the grass, the
squealer, the snitch, (call
him what you will), in order
to assist in their investiga
tions and arrests; and amaz
ingly, this is the area that
seldom gets written about."

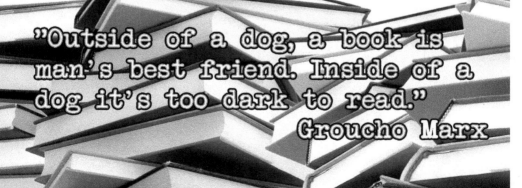

"Outside of a dog, a book is
man's best friend. Inside of a
dog it's too dark to read."
Groucho Marx

Bill Harkleroad joined Captain Beef
heart's Magic Band at a time when they
were changing from a straight ahead
blues band into something completely dif
ferent. Through the vision of Don Van
Vliet (Captain Beefheart) they created a
new form of music which many at the time
considered atonal and difficult, but
which over the years has continued to
exert a powerful influence. Beefheart re
christened Harkleroad as Zoot Horn Rollo,
and they embarked on recording one of
the classic rock albums of all time
Trout Mask Replica - a work of unequalled
daring and inventiveness.

Politics, paganism and …. Vlad
the Impaler. Selected stories
from CJ Stone from 2003 to the
present. Meet Ivor Coles, a
British Tommy killed in action
in September 1915, lost, and then
found again. Visit Mothers Club
in Erdington, the best psyche
delic music club in the UK in
the '60s. Celebrate Robin Hood's
Day and find out what a huckle
duckle is. Travel to Stonehenge
at the Summer Solstice and
carouse with the hippies. Find
out what a Ranter is, and why
CJ Stone thinks that he's one.
Take LSD with Dr Lilly, the
psychedelic scientist. Meet a
headless soldier or the ghost of
Elvis Presley in Gabalfa,
Cardiff. Journey to Whitstable,
to New York, to Malta and to
Transylvania, and to many other
places, real and imagined, polit
ical and spiritual, transcendent
and mundane. As The Independent
says, Chris is "The best guide to
the underground since Charon
ferried dead souls across the
Styx."

This is is the first in the
highly acclaimed vampire
novels of the late Mick Farren.
Victor Renquist, a surprisingly
urbane and likable leader of a
colony of vampires which has
existed for centuries in New
York is faced with both admin
istrative and emotional prob
lems. And when you are a
vampire, administration is not
a thing which one takes
lightly.

"The person, be it gentleman or
lady, who has not pleasure in a
good novel, must be intolerably
stupid."

Jane Austen